50 Thematic Songs
Sung to Your Favorite Tunes
Teach & Delight Every Child With Playful Songs
That Are Fun to Sing & a Snap to Learn!

by Meish Goldish

SCHOLASTIC
PROFESSIONAL BOOKS

NEW YORK • TORONTO • LONDON • AUCKLAND • SYDNEY
MEXICO CITY • NEW DELHI • HONG KONG

Cover design by Norma Ortiz
Cover illustration by Jane Conteh-Morgan
Interior design by Solutions by Design, Inc.
Interior illustration by Sue Dennen

ISBN 0-439-06162-8

Table of Contents

Introduction

Welcome to **50 Thematic Songs**. Integrating these 50 irresistible, songs set to familiar, kid-friendly tunes is simple, fast—and fun!

The song topics are organized by progression through the school year and by theme, making it easy to celebrate the seasons, holidays, animals, children and much more. Engaging and easy to use, the songs are an ideal supplement for introducing or reinforcing year-round thematic learning.

The songs themselves can be presented in a variety of ways. For example, you might copy them onto large chart paper, prepare transparencies for the overhead projector, or provide students with individual photocopies. You can invite children to add their own illustrations to chart paper as a class project, or you can have them illustrate a specific section of a song on their own. Children can also be encouraged to choreograph their own hand movements to correspond with a particular song, and then perform their work in front of a small group or the entire class.

Besides using the songs to reinforce specific themes you can use them during circle time to provide children with a joyous, sing-along, shared reading experience in which all children can feel successful. As with all read-aloud poems or rhyming songs, they are also a wonderful tool for teaching early literacy skills including concepts of print and words, language patterns and rhymes, and connecting sound to print.

To get the most instructional benefit from the songs in this book, we suggest that you familiarize yourself with the songs and their tunes before you begin. If possible, find the original song or tune upon which the song in this book is based. Play the original for your children so they can familiarize themselves with the music. Then invite children to sing the songs together or in small groups. You might divide the class into groups and assign each a different verse of a song. Have each group sing its verse aloud, then have the groups sing the entire song again in a round. Ask children to add their own

verses or write their own original versions of each song. Invitations to add a prop or play a simple musical instrument will spark further creativity.

Familiarizing yourself with the songs ahead of time will also allow you to approach them with greater creativity and enrich learning. For example:

- When studying colors, you might pass out sheets of construction paper of different colors. Have children hold up their individual color as it is sung in the song. Then have children illustrate those items mentioned in the song on their respective pieces of paper.

- When studying shapes, encourage children to bring to class some of the items mentioned in the song. Then divide the class into groups, assigning each to a different shape. Have them go on a *Shape Hunt* around the classroom, looking for items that have their assigned shape. Later, have each group present their findings to the class.

- When studying a memorial holiday, allow children extra time to read further about a particular historical figure. Ask them to share one fact they've learned with the class. Or, have the class participate in a collaborative research project.

- When studying songs such as "Pets," take a survey in the class to determine what kinds of pets children would want to have. Display the results in a bar graph and ask children questions about it.

Nearly all of these songs lend themselves to similar cross-curricular activities. Though there are many ways to approach and use this book, there's only one rule to follow: Have fun!

September

(sung to "Oh, Susanna!")

When we reach the end of summer,
And it's time to start the fall,
I remember it's September,
My favorite month of all!

When we all go back to school,
Back to work, and back to play,
I remember it's September,
The time for Labor Day!

CHORUS:

**Oh, September,
That's the month for me!
I remember it's September,
And I'm happy as can be!**

When I see a corn or wheat field
Growing very, very tall,
I remember it's September,
My favorite month of all!

When the farmers go to harvest,
And the harvest moon is bright,
I remember it's September,
A time that feels so right!

CHORUS

Back to School

(sung to "Over the River and through the Woods")

Late in the summer, before the fall,
It's back to school we go!
We get on the bus, which carries us
To a building we all know!
Late in the summer, before the fall,
To class we all return.
Vacation was fun, but now it's done,
And now it's time to learn!

Late in the summer, before the fall,
It's back to school we go!
The teacher is there beside her chair,
And gives a big "Hello!"
Late in the summer, before the fall,
I find the desk for me.
The year is new, new things to do!
I'm happy as can be!

Late in the summer, before the fall,
It's back to school we go!
We get new books, how nice each looks!
And soon we'll read, I know!
Late in the summer, before the fall,
I'm back in class with friends!
The school year brings exciting things,
I hope it never ends!

Apple Picking

(sung to "Camptown Races")

There's a fruit we love to eat,
Apples! Apples!
We can pick this special treat
At apple-picking time!

In the summer or the fall,
Apples! Apples!
We can have ourselves a ball
At apple-picking time!

CHORUS:

**Climbing up a tree,
A basket at my side!
I pick the nicest apples
That the apple tree's supplied!**

Some are red and some are green,
Apples! Apples!
Juiciest I've ever seen,
At apple-picking time!

Why pick apples? Tell you why:
Apples! Apples!
Applesauce and apple pie,
At apple-picking time!

CHORUS

October

(sung to "On Top of Old Smoky")

The month is October,
The air's turning cold.
The leaves are all changing
To red and to gold.

The month is October,
And up in the sky,
The birds are all traveling,
And south they will fly!

The month is October,
There's so much to do:
Play football and hockey,
And pick apples, too!

The month is October,
And ghosts I have seen.
They're out trick-or-treating,
It's now Halloween!

Christopher Columbus

(sung to "My Bonnie Lies Over the Ocean")

Columbus sailed over the ocean,
Columbus sailed over the sea,
Columbus sailed over the ocean,
An eager explorer was he!

CHORUS:

Sail on, sail on,
Columbus sailed over the sea, you see!
Sail on, sail on,
Columbus sailed over the sea!

In Spain, many people were laughing.
They said, "He'll fall flat off the earth!"
Columbus said, "I'll find the Indies!"
And sailed on for all he was worth!

CHORUS

Columbus soon came to an island,
With Native Americans there.
Columbus had sailed to the New World,
And so he explored everywhere!

CHORUS

Columbus did not find the Indies,
But land others found long before.
But still we remember Columbus,
Who followed his dream to explore!

CHORUS

Halloween

(sung to "Here We Go Looby Loo")

CHORUS:

**Here we go trick-or-treat,
Here we go out to fright!
Here we go trick-or-treat,
All on a Halloween night!**

I'm dressed up like a ghost,
In a sheet of white,
I'm dressed up like a ghost
All on a Halloween night!

CHORUS

I've got my goody bag,
It's filled with such delight!
I've got my goody bag
All on a Halloween night!

CHORUS

I see a pumpkin face,
Its glow is very bright!
I see a pumpkin face
All on a Halloween night!

CHORUS

November

(sung to "Do You Know the Muffin Man?")

CHORUS:

**Do you know November's here,
November's here, November's here?
Do you know November's here?
A great time of the year!**

Leaves are turning red and brown,
Many leaves are falling down,
Leaves have blown all over town,
A great time of the year!

CHORUS

See the squirrels run around,
Finding nuts upon the ground,
Storing up the nuts they've found,
For winter time is near!

CHORUS

Each Thanksgiving means a lot,
Let's give thanks for what we've got,
We can dance the turkey trot,
A great time of the year!

CHORUS

50 Thematic Piggyback Songs Scholastic Professional Books

Pumpkin

(sung to "Found a Peanut")

Found a pumpkin, found a pumpkin,
Found a pumpkin on a vine.
Yes, today I found a pumpkin,
And the pumpkin now is mine!

Tried to lift it, tried to lift it,
Tried to lift it off the ground.
I could hardly lift my pumpkin
For it was so big and round!

Cut it open, cut it open,
Cut it open very wide.
And I saw inside my pumpkin
All the seeds it had inside!

Scooped the inside, scooped the inside,
Scooped the inside, me oh my!
Cooked the inside of my pumpkin,
And I ate sweet pumpkin pie!

Thanksgiving Day

(sung to "Row, Row, Row Your Boat")

Show, show, show your thanks,
In a special way,
Celebrate, celebrate, celebrate, celebrate
On Thanksgiving Day!

Show, show, show your thanks,
Let your thanks include
Family, family, family, family
For your clothes and food!

Show, show, show your thanks,
Thanks to all your friends.
On friendship, friendship, friendship, friendship,
Everyone depends!

Show, show, show your thanks
As in Pilgrim days.
On Thanksgiving show your thanks
In many, many ways!

50 Thematic Piggyback Songs Scholastic Professional Books

December

(sung to "I've Been Working on the Railroad")

I've been waiting for December,
All the long, long year.
I've been waiting for December,
And at last it's finally here!
Now the autumn time is over,
Winter has come to take its place.
Snow is falling all around me,
With snowflakes on my face!

I've been waiting for December,
For a whole year long.
I've been waiting for December
Just to sing a holiday song!
Christmas, Hanukkah, and Kwanzaa,
New Year's Eve is here, oh boy!
Let's all celebrate December,
A month of fun and joy!

Hibernation

(sung to "London Bridge Is Falling Down")

CHORUS:

Animals are not around,
Not around, not around.
Animals are not around:
They're hibernating!

In the winter, where's the bear?
In a den, in a lair.
Till the spring, it's sleeping there:
It's hibernating!

In the winter, where's the frog?
In a pond, or a log.
It won't hop, and it won't jog!
It's hibernating!

CHORUS

In the winter, where's the bat?
In a cave is where it's at.
It is sleeping. Why is that?
It's hibernating!

In the winter, where's the snake?
In the mud, in the lake.
Sleeping through its winter break:
It's hibernating!

CHORUS

50 Thematic Piggyback Songs Scholastic Professional Books

January

(sung to "Alouette")

CHORUS:

**January, first is January,
January, first month of the year!**

In this month is New Year's Day,
Happy New Year! Hip hooray!
New Year's Day! Hip hooray! Oh!

CHORUS

In this month it's very cold,
Frosty winds are oh so bold!
Very cold! Oh so bold!
New Year's Day! Hip hooray! Oh!

CHORUS

In this month we proudly sing
Of Dr. Martin Luther King!
Proudly sing! Dr. King!
Very cold! Oh so bold!
New Year's Day! Hip hooray! Oh!

CHORUS

In this month let's give a cheer,
First month of a brand new year!
Give a cheer! Brand new year!
Proudly sing! Dr. King!
Very cold! Oh so bold!
New Year's Day! Hip hooray! Oh!

CHORUS

February

(sung to "Yankee Doodle")

In the month of February,
I'm so very glad! Oh,
The groundhog comes on Groundhog Day
A-looking for his shadow!

February, what a month!
Cold and crisp and snowy,
Middle of the winter when
The winds are sharp and blowy!

Presidents' Day in February
Always sets me thinkin'
About our special pair of heroes:
Washington and Lincoln!

February, what a month!
Filled with lots of cheer now!
Will you be my Valentine?
Valentine's Day is here now!

50 Thematic Piggyback Songs Scholastic Professional Books

Valentine's Day

(sung to "Lullaby and Good Night")

Please be mine,
Valentine,
You're the one that I care for!
Here's my heart
Drawn in art,
It's especially drawn for you!
Just in case
You like lace,
There is lace on the lining,
Pink and white,
Nice and bright,
All especially made for you!

Please be mine,
Valentine,
You're a friend that I cherish!
Here's a sweet
Chocolate treat
I especially got for you!
Be my friend,
And we'll spend
All our free time together!
Valentine,
Please be mine,
I'm especially fond of you!

100th Day of School

(sung to "Ninety-Nine Bottles of Beer on the Wall")

100 days of school in all,
100 days of school,
We managed to count a large amount,
100 days of school in all!

How did we get 100 days?
100 days of school?
We started the fun with number 1,
Counting the days of school in all!

1 day of school at first,
Then 2, then 3, then 4.
We got up to 10, but didn't stop then,
We went to 100 days in all!

20, 30, 40 days,
50 days and more!
60, 70, 80, 90,
Up to 100 days in all!

100 days of school in all,
100 days of school,
We managed to count a large amount,
100 days of school in all!

50 Thematic Piggyback Songs Scholastic Professional Books

March

(sung to "The Ants Come Marching One By One")

The month of March is marching in,
Hurrah, hurrah!
The month of March, let spring begin,
Hurrah, hurrah!
The month of March is marching in,
And birds return from where they've been,
And we all feel good
When March is marching in!

The month of March is turning warm,
Hurrah, hurrah!
And tiny buds begin to form,
Hurrah, hurrah!
The month of March is turning warm,
And bugs and bees begin to swarm,
And we all feel good
When March is marching in!

The month of March brings happy days,
Hurrah, hurrah!
We celebrate in many ways,
Hurrah, hurrah!
The month of March brings happy days,
St. Patrick's Day has great parades,
And we all feel good
When March is marching in!

April

(sung to "Daisy, Daisy")

April, April,
Days may be warm or cool,
Let's have fun but
Don't be an April Fool!
We'll work on our garden flowers,
And watch for April showers,
On Arbor Day
We'll sing and play
As we plant a new tree at school!

April, April,
Time for a holiday,
Easter bunny
Hopping along the way!
The leaves on the trees are growing,
The farmers now are hoeing,
It's green, it's spring,
It's time to sing
Now that April is here to stay!

May

(sung to "Polly-Wolly-Doodle All the Day")

Oh, the sun is out, it's fun to play,
In the merry, merry month of May!
Let's watch the flowers dance and sway
In the merry, merry month of May!

CHORUS:

All is well, all is well,
All is well each merry day!
All the plants are growing,
Their colors are showing
In the merry, merry month of May!

Such happy days all come our way
In the merry, merry month of May!
I'll hug my mom on Mother's Day
In the merry, merry month of May.

It's Cinco de Mayo, shout "Ole!"
In the merry, merry month of May!
And don't forget Memorial Day
In the merry, merry month of May!

CHORUS

June

(sung to "Skip to My Lou")

CHORUS:

June, June, hooray, it's June!
June, June, hooray, it's June!
June, June, hooray, it's June!
June is the start of summer!

Days are hot, and school is out,
Birds and bees are all about,
Blooming roses make me shout,
June is the start of summer!

CHORUS

Flag Day makes me feel so proud,
Flags are waving in a crowd,
Let's salute and shout out loud,
June is the start of summer!

CHORUS

Father's Day at last is here,
Hug a dad and give a cheer,
It's my favorite time of year,
June is the start of summer!

CHORUS

50 Thematic Piggyback Songs Scholastic Professional Books

All About Me

(sung to "For He's a Jolly Good Fellow")

CHORUS:

Oh, I'm a wonderful person,
I'm a wonderful person,
I'm a wonderful person,
And very special, too!

In how I dress and look,
In what's my favorite book!

CHORUS

In how I write my name,
In what's my favorite game!

CHORUS

In things I eat and drink,
In things I like to think!

CHORUS

In how I laugh and talk,
In how I run and walk.

CHORUS

In songs I like to sing,
In fact, in *everything!*

CHORUS

Families

(sung to "Oh Dear, What Can the Matter Be?")

CHORUS:

Tell me, what is a family?
Tell me, how many can there be?
Tell me, whose is a family?
Families come in all kinds!

Some may have fathers, some may have mothers,
And some may have sisters, some may have brothers,
And some may have cousins, some may have others,
Yes, families come in all kinds!

CHORUS

Some families are big, some families are smaller,
Some families are short, some families are taller,
Just like different coins can make up a dollar,
A family is made of all kinds!

CHORUS

50 Thematic Piggyback Songs Scholastic Professional Books

Friends

(sung to "This Old Man, He Played One")

I'm a friend, so are you,
Friendship is like special glue,
'Cause we stick together, never fall apart,
Friendship is a special art!

We are friends, night and day,
Friends at work, and friends at play,
Doesn't matter if we're happy or we're sad,
Friendship always makes us glad!

We can laugh, we can sing,
Oh what joys that friends can bring!
When you've got a friend, you really are complete,
Friendship is a special treat!

Friends like us always share,
Sharing shows how much we care!
We can share a snack, a story, or a toy,
Friendship brings us special joy!

I'm a friend, so are you,
Friendship is like special glue,
'Cause we stick together, never fall apart,
Friendship is a special art!

Happy Birthday!

(sung to "If You're Happy and You Know It")

If you're happy on your birthday, tell your friends!
If you're happy on your birthday, tell your friends!
If you're happy on this day,
Shout a happy, "Hip hooray!"
If you're happy on your birthday, tell your friends!

If you're happy on your birthday, eat some cake!
If you're happy on your birthday, eat some cake!
Eat some cake that tastes delish,
Blow the candles, make a wish!
If you're happy on your birthday, eat some cake!

If you're happy on your birthday, read your cards!
If you're happy on your birthday, read your cards!
Every card you get, it's true,
Sends a birthday wish to you!
If you're happy on your birthday, read your cards!

If you're happy on your birthday, have some fun!
If you're happy on your birthday, have some fun!
Throw a party, play a game,
Sing a song that has your name!
If you're happy on your birthday, have some fun!

50 Thematic Piggyback Songs Scholastic Professional Books

I Lost a Tooth

(sung to "Ta-Ra-Ra-Boom-De-Ay")

Ta-ra-ra-boom-de-ay!
I lost my tooth today!
When I went out to play,
It just fell out that way!
Ta-ra-ra-boom-de-ay!
I lost my tooth today!
Now I would like to say,
Hip hip hooray!

Ta-ra-ra-boom-de-ay!
I lost my tooth today!
I know that it's okay,
'Cause baby teeth don't stay!
Ta-ra-ra-boom-de-ay!
New teeth will come my way!
They'll grow in any day!
Hip hip hooray!

Know Your ABCs

(sung to "The Alphabet Song")

A B C D E F G,
Letters help both you and me.
All the words we ever see
Need those letters just to be!
ABC to XYZ,
So important, you'll agree!

A is airplane, **B** is bat,
C is cozy, curly cat,
D is dinner, **E** is eat,
F is fox's furry feet,
G is garden, **H** is ham,
I is ice cream, **J** is jam.

K is kitchen, **L** is lake,
M is messes monkeys make,
N is neighbor, **O** is owl,
P is panther on the prowl,
Q is quarter, **R** is rug,
S is snail, and **T** is tug.

U is uncle, **V** is van,
W is window fan,
X is X-ray, **Y** is you,
Z is zebra in the zoo.
You can spell a word with ease,
If you know your **ABC**s!

50 Thematic Piggyback Songs Scholastic Professional Books

Numbers

(sung to "Ten Little Indians")

CHORUS:

1 little, 2 little, 3 little numbers,
4 little, 5 little, 6 little numbers,
7 little, 8 little, 9 little numbers,
10 little numbers help me count!

I'm 1 person, you make 2,
And 3 are he and I and you,
Here comes one more, so now we're 4,
Yes, these little numbers help me count!

CHORUS

5 are fingers on my hand,
And 6 guitar strings in a band,
And 7 days a week are grand,
Yes, these little numbers help me count!

CHORUS

8 arms on those octopi,
9 planets in the solar sky,
10 pennies make a dime, oh my!
Yes, these little numbers help me count!

CHORUS

Colors

(sung to "Sing a Song of Sixpence")

Sing a song of red,
A cherry so sweet.
Sing a song of purple,
Fresh plums to eat.
Sing a song of green,
A pear or a pea.
Sing a song of yellow,
Pass the buttered corn to me!

Sing a song of white,
Some milk and some rice.
Sing a song of brown,
Hot chocolate is nice.
Sing a song of blue,
A blueberry pie.
Sing a song of orange,
Have a peach, and so will I!

50 Thematic Piggyback Songs Scholastic Professional Books

Shapes

(sung to "When the Saints Go Marching In")

CHORUS:

Look at the shape that things are in,
Look at the shape that things are in,
Look at the sides and top and bottom,
Look at the shape that things are in!

A shiny dime, a big balloon,
A wagon wheel, a full, round moon.
All of these things are shaped like a **circle,**
Look at the shape these things are in!

A TV screen, a slice of cheese,
A napkin just in case you sneeze!
All of these things are shaped like a **square,**
Look at the shape these things are in!

A kitchen door, a cozy bed,
A dollar bill, a loaf of bread.
All of these things are shaped like a **rectangle,**
Look at the shape these things are in!

A piece of pie with sides of three,
A pizza slice for you and me.
All of these things are shaped like a **triangle,**
Look at the shape these things are in!

CHORUS

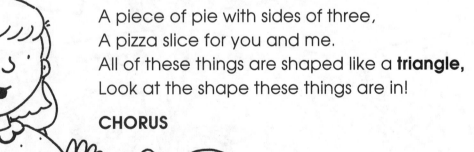

Days of the Week

(sung to "Rock-a-Bye Baby in the Treetop")

Busy on Monday,
Reading a book.
Busy on Tuesday,
Helping to cook.
Busy on Wednesday,
Letters to write,
Busy on Thursday,
Flying my kite.

Busy on Friday,
Riding my bike,
Busy on Saturday,
Taking a hike.
Busy on Sunday,
Singing a song,
I am so busy
All the week long!

50 Thematic Piggyback Songs Scholastic Professional Books

Four Seasons
(sung to "The Farmer in the Dell")

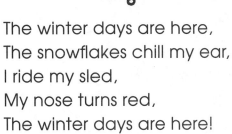

The winter days are here,
The snowflakes chill my ear,
I ride my sled,
My nose turns red,
The winter days are here!

The springtime now is here,
It's warm, and skies are clear,
The birds and bees
Are in the trees,
The springtime now is here.

The summer days are here,
The hottest time of year,
I swim a lot
Because I'm hot,
The summer days are here.

The days of fall are here,
And golden leaves appear,
They fall from trees
When there's a breeze,
The days of fall are here!

Five Senses

(sung to "Frère Jacques")

Are you looking? Are you seeing?
Use your eyes! Use your eyes!
Whenever you are looking,
whenever you are seeing,
Use your eyes! Use your eyes!

Are you hearing? Are you listening?
Use your ears! Use your ears!
Whenever you are hearing,
whenever you are listening,
Use your ears! Use your ears!

Are you touching? Are you feeling?
Use your hands! Use your hands!
Whenever you are touching,
whenever you are feeling,
Use your hands! Use your hands!

Are you eating? Are you tasting?
Use your tongue! Use your tongue!
Whenever you are eating,
whenever you are tasting,
Use your tongue! Use your tongue!

Are you sniffing? Are you smelling?
Use your nose! Use your nose!
Whenever you are sniffing,
whenever you are smelling,
Use your nose! Use your nose!

50 Thematic Piggyback Songs Scholastic Professional Books

Feelings

(sung to "Hokey Pokey")

I'm having fun in school,
I'm with a friend at play,
I'm swimming in the pool,
And I'm **happy** all the day!
I've got a certain feeling,
It's a feeling that I feel—
That's what I'm all about!

I lost a baseball game,
I made my brother mad,
I broke a picture frame,
And I'm feeling kind of **sad!**
I've got a certain feeling,
It's a feeling that I feel—
That's what I'm all about!

I hear the thunder boom,
I see some bugs invade,
I'm in a darkened room,
And I'm feeling so **afraid!**
I've got a certain feeling,
It's a feeling that I feel—
That's what I'm all about!

Yes, there are times I'm up,
There are times I'm down,
There are times I smile,
There are times I tend to frown!
I've got a lot of **feelings**,
They're the feelings that I feel—
That's what I'm all about!

Weather

(sung to "It Ain't Gonna' Rain No More, No More")

It is gonna' be a **rainy** day,
It is a rainy day,
When clouds of gray all come your way,
It is gonna' be a rainy day!

It is gonna' be a **sunny** day,
It is a sunny day,
When rays of light are shining bright,
It is gonna' be a sunny day!

It is gonna' be a **windy** day,
It is a windy day,
When strong winds blow you to and fro,
It is gonna' be a windy day!

It is gonna' be a **snowy** day,
It is a snowy day,
When snowflakes fall, both big and small,
It is gonna' be a snowy day!

What is the **weather** like today?
What's it like today?
Rain or sun or wind or snow,
What is the weather like today?

50 Thematic Piggyback Songs Scholastic Professional Books

Rain Forest Animals

(sung to "Take Me out to the Ball Game")

Take me into the rain forest,
Take me into the green.
Show me the monkeys up in the trees,
Show me butterflies, parrots, and bees!

Let me look, look, look for a tiger,
With coat of yellow and gold,
For it's fun to see all the creatures
Our rain forests hold!

Take me into the rain forest,
Take me under the leaves,
Lizards and pythons are on the ground,
Sloths are hanging from trees upside down!

Let me look, look, look for a toucan,
With beak of red, blue, and green.
Yes, it's fun to see all the rain forest
Sights I've seen!

Ocean Life

(sung to "Down by the Station")

Out in the ocean,
Swimming in the water,
See the many fishes
In the open sea:
Up leaps a marlin,
Down dives a tuna,
Here come the clown fish,
Happy as can be!

Out in the ocean,
Swimming in the water,
See the many creatures
In the open sea:
Here comes a blue whale,
There goes a white shark,
Look at the dolphins,
Happy as can be!

Out in the ocean,
Resting in the water,
See the many creatures
On the ocean floor:
There sits a snail and
There sits an oyster,
There sits a clam,
And many, many more!

50 Thematic Piggyback Songs Scholastic Professional Books

Whales

(sung to "The Wheels on the Bus")

The whales in the sea are very big,
Very big, very big!
The whales in the sea are very big,
Oh, see the whales!

The whales in the sea move up and down,
Up and down, up and down,
The whales in the sea move up and down,
Oh, see the whales!

The whales in the sea have fins and tails,
Fins and tails, fins and tails!
The whales in the sea have fins and tails,
Oh, see the whales!

The whales in the sea breathe through a spout,
Through a spout, through a spout!
The whales in the sea breathe through a spout,
Oh, see the whales!

Penguin

(sung to "I'm a Little Teapot")

I'm a little penguin,
Two feet high.
I am a bird,
But I can't fly.
Look at how I swim
Out in the sea:
I'm as fast
As fast can be!

I'm a little penguin,
White and black,
White on my front,
And black in back.
Look at how I waddle
By the sea:
I'm as cute
As cute can be!

50 Thematic Piggyback Songs Scholastic Professional Books

Pets

(sung to "Mary Had a Little Lamb")

CHORUS:
If you could get a little pet,
Little pet, little pet,
If you could get a little pet,
Which pet would you get?

You can teach a dog some tricks,
Stay and sit! Fetch a stick!
You can teach a dog some tricks,
A dog can be your pet!

You can rub a cat's soft fur,
See her curl! Hear her purr!
You can rub a cat's soft fur,
A cat can be your pet!

CHORUS

You can watch a fish all day,
See him swim! See him play!
You can watch a fish all day,
A fish can be your pet!

You can feed a bird some seed,
Watch her fly! Watch her feed!
You can feed a bird some seed,
A bird can be your pet!

CHORUS

Bear

(sung to "The Old Gray Mare")

The great big bear is
Out in the autumn time,
Eating a lot of fish,
Eating a lot of fruit.
The great big bear is
Out in the autumn time,
Eating up all it can!

The great big bear knows
Winter is coming soon,
So he is getting fat,
My, he is getting fat!
The great big bear knows
Winter is coming soon,
And he will hibernate!

The great big bear crawls
Into his cozy den,
There he will stay until
Springtime is here again!
The great big bear crawls
Into his cozy den,
Sleeping all winter long!
Shhhh!

50 Thematic Piggyback Songs Scholastic Professional Books

Bat

(sung to "Where Have You Been, Billy Boy?")

Tell me, where have you been,
Little bat, little bat?
Tell me, where have you been
All the daytime?

I've been sleeping all the day,
Upside down—my favorite way!
As I wait for the skies
To turn to gray time!

Tell me, where have you been,
Little bat, little bat?
Tell me, where have you been
All the nighttime?

I've been flying all the night,
Catching insects for a bite!
I'll return to my cave
When it is light time!

Farm Animals

(sung to "Here We Go Round the Mulberry Bush")

CHORUS:

Here we go round the animal farm,
The animal farm, the animal farm.
Here we go round the animal farm
To see the barnyard creatures!

Pigs and hogs are in their pens,
In the coops are chicks and hens,
Turkeys, geese, and ducks are friends
Among the barnyard creatures!

CHORUS

In the meadow are the sheep,
Donkeys run and horses leap,
Cows are standing fast asleep,
Among the barnyard creatures!

CHORUS

A rooster's hopping with a hare,
Goats are roaming here and there,
Animals are everywhere
Among the barnyard creatures!

CHORUS

50 Thematic Piggyback Songs Scholastic Professional Books

Eggs

(sung to "Hush Little Baby, Don't Say a Word")

Hush, little baby, don't say a word,
You're inside the egg laid by your mama bird.

Mama bird's sitting on the egg in her nest,
Giving you a chance to grow and rest.

The egg protects you very well,
Safely inside a hardened shell.

Baby, be patient! Just you wait.
Your egg needs time to incubate.

Now your egg is ready to crack,
It's time to hatch, yes that's a fact.

Out pops your head, and out pops a leg,
Look, baby bird! You've hatched from your egg!

Dinosaurs

(sung to "Where, Oh Where Has My Little Dog Gone?")

CHORUS:

Oh where, oh where have the dinosaurs gone?
Oh where, oh where can they be?
Long ago, these giants ruled over the earth,
But now, not one do we see!

The dinosaurs were as tall as the trees,
And chewed the leaves at the top.
They ate plants and meat, and so much they would eat,
They'd eat, and never would stop!

CHORUS

The dinosaurs lived all over the earth:
The woods, the mountains, the sea.
They were here and there, they were most everywhere,
Around the world they would be!

CHORUS

The dinosaurs now have all disappeared,
At last, they've all said goodbye.
Though, they once were giants, they now are extinct,
And no one really knows why!

CHORUS

50 Thematic Piggyback Songs Scholastic Professional Books

Butterfly Life Cycle

(sung to "Miss Lucy Had a Baby")

The butterfly is happy,
She's laid all of her eggs.
Out pops a caterpillar
Crawling on its legs.

The baby caterpillar
Is very, very thin.
But then it eats and eats until
It bursts right through its skin!

Soon the caterpillar
Has grown so very big.
So next the caterpillar
Climbs on a leaf or twig.

The caterpillar makes a shell,
And there it hangs inside.
In time the shell starts cracking,
And soon the parts divide.

The shell is nearly open,
Wow! It's really strange!
The caterpillar in the shell
Has undergone a change!

Now that the shell is open,
Look what's coming out:
A fully grown butterfly
Is fluttering about!

Spider

(sung to "The Eensy Weensy Spider")

The eensy weensy spider
Crawls up the kitchen wall.
Its very hairy legs
Help the spider not to fall.
It's crawled into a corner
At the very top,
Where the eensy weensy spider
Can stay and never drop.

The eensy weensy spider
Is hanging in the air.
It spins a web of silk
That runs from here to there.
When the web is finished,
The spider has a grin,
And the eensy weensy spider
Says, "Bugs, please come right in!"

50 Thematic Piggyback Songs Scholastic Professional Books

Bugs

(sung to "Little Brown Jug")

CHORUS:

Ha ha ha, hee hee hee,
Little brown bug, who can you be?
Ha ha ha, hee hee hee,
Little brown bug, who can you be?

Who's that creeping in the grass?
See the beetle slowly pass!
Who's that crawling across my pants?
It's a band of marching ants!

CHORUS

Who's that leaping off the ground?
Hop, grasshopper! Hop around!
Who's that flying close to me?
It's a busy honeybee!

CHORUS

Who's that lighting up the dark?
Fireflies are in the park!
Who's that buzzing near my ear?
Shoo, mosquito, out of here!

CHORUS

Homes

(sung to "This Land Is Your Land")

CHORUS:

This home is your home,
That home is my home,
Some have a low home,
Some have a high home.
From a small apartment
To a giant palace,
This world has different homes to see!

Some live in igloos,
Some have a tepee,
Some stay in camp tents
When they are sleepy!
Some have a houseboat
Or a simple straw hut,
This world has different homes to see!

CHORUS

Some choose a cabin,
A simple log house,
My puppy Rover
Lives in a doghouse!
Whether a castle
Or an adobe,
This world has different homes to see!

CHORUS

50 Thematic Piggyback Songs Scholastic Professional Books

Neighborhood Helpers

(sung to "Goodnight, Ladies")

CHORUS:

**Hello, neighbors, hello, neighbors,
Hello, neighbors, you help in many ways!**

Bakers bake the food we eat,
Food we eat, food we eat!
Grocers sell the food we eat,
They help in many ways!

CHORUS

Teachers help us learn a lot,
Learn a lot, learn a lot!
Librarians help us read a lot,
They help in many ways!

CHORUS

Doctors help to keep us well,
Keep us well, keep us well!
Nurses help to keep us well,
They help in many ways!

CHORUS

Firefighters and police are there
To keep us safe everywhere!
Firefighters and police are there,
They help in many ways!

CHORUS

Ways to Travel

(sung to "Sailing, Sailing, Over the Bounding Main")

Sailing, sailing,
Out on a sea or lake,
When traveling by water,
A boat is what you take!
Flying, flying,
High up in the air.
To travel far and travel fast,
A plane can get you there!

Driving, driving,
Driving near or far,
A good way you can go by road
Is by driving in a car!
Riding, riding,
Riding without a fuss!
If you don't want to take a car,
You can ride the bus!

Chugging, chugging,
Chugging along the track,
Riding on a railroad train
Can get you there and back!
Walking, walking,
Walking along the ground,
For shorter trips, just use your feet
To get yourself around!

50 Thematic Piggyback Songs Scholastic Professional Books

Night Sky

(sung to "Twinkle Twinkle, Little Star")

Twinkle, twinkle, little star,
In the night sky, there you are.
Next to you I see the moon,
Like a giant white balloon!
Twinkle, twinkle, moon and star,
In the night sky, there you are!

Hooting, hooting, little owl,
In the night you're on the prowl!
Sky so dark, yet you can see,
Watching high up in a tree.
Hooting, hooting, little owl,
In the night you're on the prowl!

Twinkle, twinkle, firefly,
Lighting up the evening sky.
In the night I see you glow,
Twinkling, then away you go!
Twinkle, twinkle, firefly,
Lighting up the evening sky!

Book Links

Heroes, Holidays, and Happy Days

January Brings the Snow: A Book of Months by Jenni Oliver, Dial, 1986.

School Days by B.G. Hennessy, Dutton Children's Books, 1995.

I Am an Apple by Jean Marzollo, Scholastic, 1997.

Red Leaf, Yellow Leaf by Lois Ehlert, Harcourt Brace & Company, 1991.

In 1492 by Jean Marzollo, Scholastic, 1991.

It's Halloween by Jack Prelutsky, Scholastic, 1987.

The Snowy Day by Ezra Jack Keats, Viking Press, 1963.

Pumpkin Pumpkin by Jeanne Titherington, Greenwillow, 1986.

Over the River and Through the Woods: A Song for Thanksgiving by Lydia Maria Child, HarperCollins, 1993.

Wake Me in Spring by James Preller, Scholastic, 1994.

Happy Birthday, Martin Luther King by Jean Marzollo, Scholastic, 1993.

George Washington by Laurence Santrey, Troll, 1982.

Miss Bindergarten Celebrates the 100th Day of Kindergarten by Joseph Slate, Dutton Children's Books, 1998.

Valentine's Day by Gail Gibbons, Holiday House, 1986.

Spring Is Here by Taro Gomi, Chronicle Books, 1999.

My Barn by Craig Brown, Greenwillow, 1991.

Me, My Friends, and I

I Like Me by Nancy Carlson, Viking Penguin, 1988.

Families Are Different by Nini Pellegrini, Holiday House, 1991.

My Friends by Taro Gomi, Chronicle Books, 1990.

It's My Birthday! by Helen Oxenbury, Candlewick, 1993.

Boots Loses a Tooth by Sara James, Smithmark, 1993.

Basic Skills Builders

Chika Chika Boom Boom by Bill Martin, Jr., & John Archambault, Simon & Schuster, 1989.

Count and See by Tana Hoban, Simon & Schuster, 1972.

Freight Train by Donald Crews, Puffin, 1985.

Shape of Things to Come by Dayle Ann Dodds, Candlewick, 1994.

Cookie's Week by Cindy Ward, Putnam, 1988.

Caps, Hats, Socks, and Mittens by Louise Borden, Scholastic, 1992.

My Five Senses by Aliki, Crowell, 1989.

Feelings by Aliki, Greenwillow, 1984.

What Will The Weather Be Like Today? by Paul Rogers, Greenwillow, 1989.

Animals Are Everywhere!

Rain Forest by Helen Cowcher, Farrar, Strauss, & Giroux, 1988.

Wonders of the Sea by Louis Sabin, Troll, 1982.

Going on a Whale Watch by Bruce McMillan, Scholastic, 1992.

Penguins by Roger T. Peterson, Houghton Mifflin Company, 1998.

An Egg Is An Egg by Nick Weiss, Putnam Publishing Group, 1996.

Bears by Ruth Krauss, Scholastic, 1968.

A Bat is Born by Randell Jarrell, Doubleday, 1978.

Pets by Dave King, Aladdin, 1991.

Giant Dinosaurs by Erna Rowe, Scholastic, 1973.

The Very Hungry Caterpillar by Eric Carle, Philomel, 1979.

I Love Spiders by John Parker, Scholastic, 1989.

Bugs! by Patricia McKissack & Frederick McKissack, Children's Press, 1988.

All Around the Neighborhood

Have You Seen Houses? by Joanne Oppenheim, Young Scott Books, 1973.

Guess Who? by Margaret Miller, Greenwillow, 1994.

Red Light Stop, Green Light Go by Andrew Kuhlman, Simon and Schuster, 1993.

The Night Sky by Alice Pernick, Scholastic, 1994.